HELLO GRIEF

I'LL BE RIGHT WITH YOU

ALESSANDRA OLANOW

HARPER DESIGN
An Imprint of HarperCollinsPublishers

FOR MOM

i'm sorry, please forgive me,
thank you, i love you.

- ho'oponopono cleansing prayer

INTRODUCTION

WHEN I LOOK BACK TO MY PERSONAL LOSS, THE SUDDEN LOSS OF MY MOTHER, I CAN INSTANTLY TRANSPORT MYSELF TO THAT SPACE OF PAIN, DISORIENTATION, AND COMPLETE HOLLOWNESS. ON THE DAY SHE DIED, I REMEMBER DRIVING BACK HOME TO BROOKLYN FROM HER BEDSIDE, ARRIVING IN MY NEIGHBORHOOD AND BEING STARTLED BY HOW THE UPS MAN WAS STILL DELIVERING PACKAGES, A COUPLE WAS LAUGHING ON THEIR WAY TO THE LOCAL COFFEE SPOT, MY NEIGHBOR WHISTLING WHILE SWEEPING HIS STOOP... HOW WAS THIS POSSIBLE, HADN'T THEY HEARD? MY MOM WAS GONE, WHY WAS LIFE STILL HAPPENING?

AND THAT IS THE PAINFUL TRUTH, LIFE GOES ON. AS MY SADNESS ENVELOPED ME, AND THE MEANING OF IT ALL BECAME SO MURKY IN MY MIND, THE WORLD AROUND ME TURNED. I FELT SO ISOLATED AND ALONE, AS IF I WAS ON THE OTHER SIDE OF SOME GLASS PANE DIVIDING ME FROM MY OLD, BLISSFULLY UNAWARE SELF. SUDDENLY, IT ALL LOOKED COMPLETELY DIFFERENT.

LOSS OR SEPARATION FROM SOMEONE OR SOMETHING WE ARE CONNECTED TO IS LIFE'S MOST DIFFICULT HURDLE. YOU HAVE TO ALLOW YOURSELF YOUR PROCESS, REMEMBERING NO TWO PEOPLE WILL GRIEVE IN THE SAME WAY.

AND IT'S NOT LIMITED TO DEATH. WE WILL GRIEVE FOR THINGS, SUCH AS OUR YOUTH, OLD RELATIONSHIPS (EVEN THE BAD ONES), HABITS (THE DESTRUCTIVE BUT NOSTALGICALLY FUN ONES), OR EVEN A FORMER IDENTITY.

THIS BOOK IS MY EXPLORATION OF GRIEVING MY MOTHER. MY JOURNEY NAVIGATING THROUGH THE COMPLEX FEELINGS OF LOSS AND LONGING TO FIND MEANING.

GRIEF IS NORMAL, OMNIPRESENT, AND NECESSARY.
PLEASE TAKE CARE AND TAKE TIME TO UNDERSTAND YOUR GRIEF, SO THAT HEALING MAY BEGIN.

♥, ALESSANDRA

part one:
heart breaks

and it all unravels

the shock and the despair,
the hopelessness, the fear,
the realization of no more *hello*s
or *see you next time*s

SUDDENLY THE WORLD
FELT UPSIDE - DOWN.

YOUR BODY MIGHT
FEEL THE LOSS
BEFORE YOUR BRAIN.

BLURRY

SHOCK

GUILT

SCARED

DIZZY

LONGING

BITTER

SELFPITY

SOMETIMES
YOU NEED
TO STAY IN
THE CLOUD

START
HERE

THE PATH

IT'S OK
TO CRY

IT'S OK
NOT TO CRY

WE GROW WILD.

my feelings grow wild.
i wrap my hand around a good one
(my instinct wants to hold tight),
but as quickly as it arrives,
that same feeling withers away,
replaced with something new.
perhaps a pain that slowly sprouts,
a heartache that circles my stomach
and finds the tip of my tongue until
it too blossoms into another emotion.

my feelings grow wild,
up and down and sideways.
how strange and unsettling
to watch them all bloom.

NOTE TO SELF,

LET ME SEE THINGS
AS THEY ARE.

I JUST
REALLY
MISS YOU

part two:
the illusion that it could have been different

ALL THE
THINGS I
WISH I SAID.

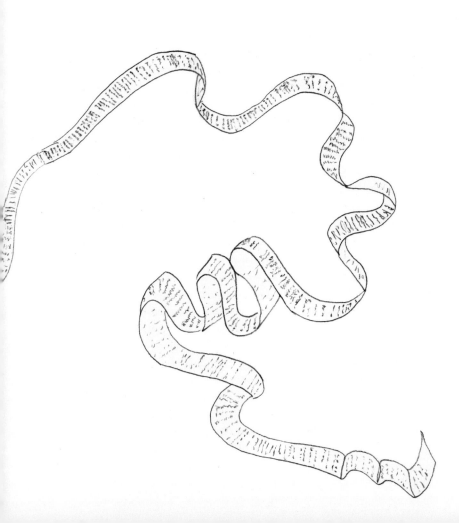

regret shows up,
an unwanted guest
urging me to examine all of the what-ifs,
i let it hold me hostage
replaying every hard moment

why did i say this
or why didn't i say that?

and i will live in this illusion
that things could be different
until my head and heart are ready
to accept that they cannot.

MAYBE IT'S
NOT HAPPENING.

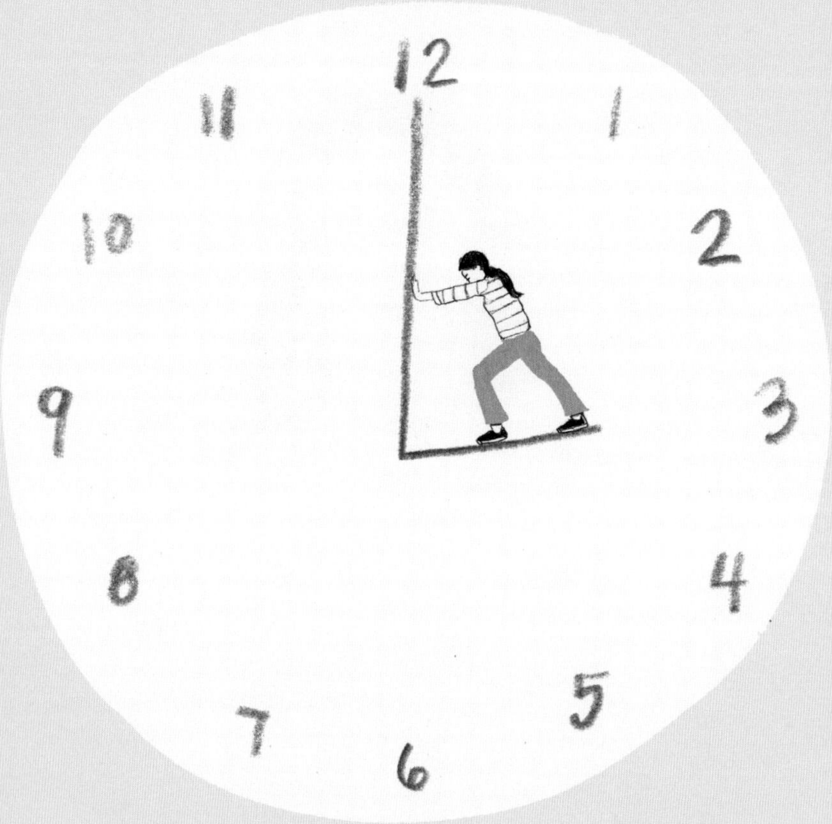
12
1
2
3
4
5
6
7
8
9
10
11

THE HARDEST PART OF FORWARD MOTION
IS THE DESIRE TO GO BACK.

WHY CAN'T IT FIT THE
WAY I WANT IT TO?

●

EVERYTHING I KNOW

EVERYTHING I DON'T KNOW

HAVE A  DAY.

SOME DAYS JUST
WON'T BE NICE.

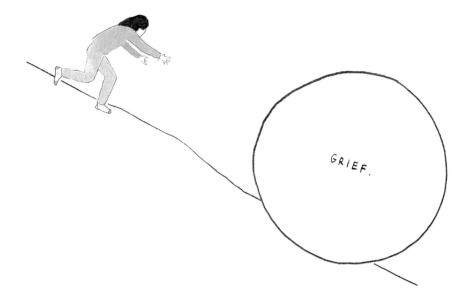

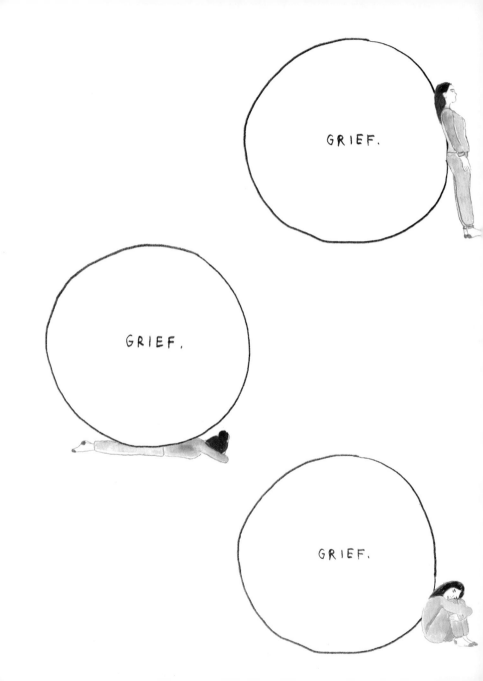

YOU'RE EVERYWHERE
EXCEPT HERE.

BUT WHEN
I MISS
SEEING YOU,

I CLOSE MY EYES.

♥

part three:
and now i isolate

allow time and space
to explore all feelings
without judgment.

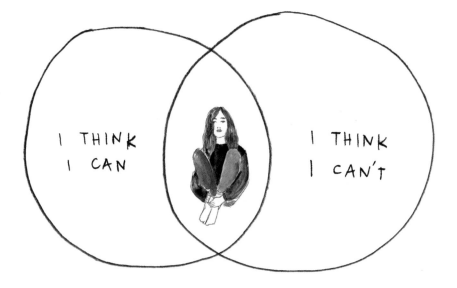

I THINK
I CAN

I THINK
I CAN'T

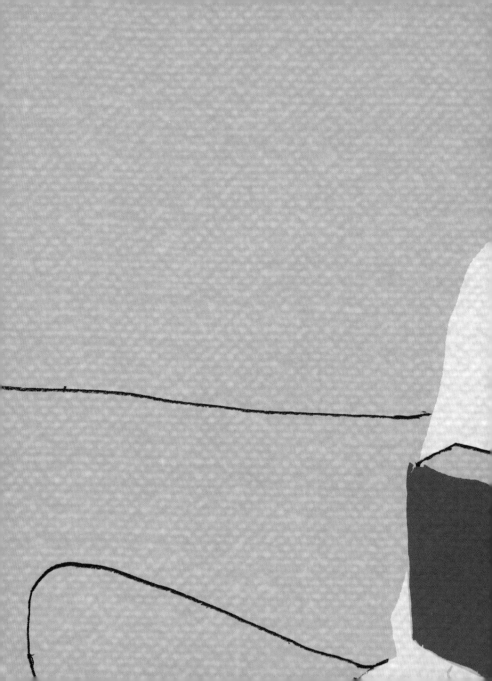

IT WILL
PROBABLY
BE FINE.

DAY PLANNER

DATE / DATE

TAKE IT
DAY BY DAY.

life is made up of planned
and unplanned changes.

let what's happening
be what's happening
until the next shift arises.

AND I TOLD THE
NIGHT EVERYTHING.

IN STILLNESS
THERE'S MOVEMENT.

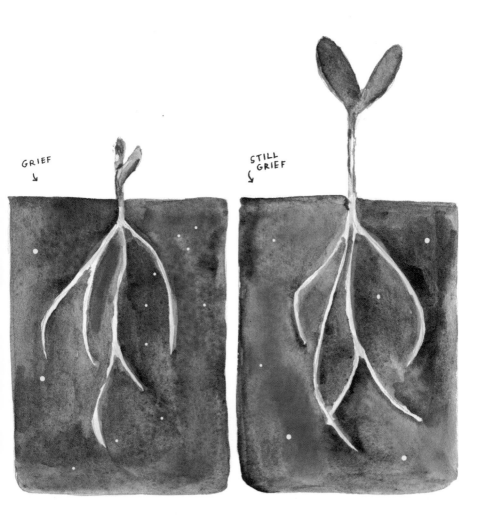

GRIEF

STILL GRIEF

TRUST YOUR ABILITY TO TRANSFORM.

SOMETIMES THERE IS BEAUTY IN
A PAIN THAT NEVER GOES AWAY.

acknowledge it.
absorb it.
let it run through you
until it becomes a part of you.
that's when the healing begins.

REMEMBER, WE ALL GRIEVE AT OUR OWN PACE.

part four:

accept. accept more.

BOTTOM IS A
GOOD PLACE TO
START.

SIT WITH YOUR FEELINGS

INHALE

EXHALE

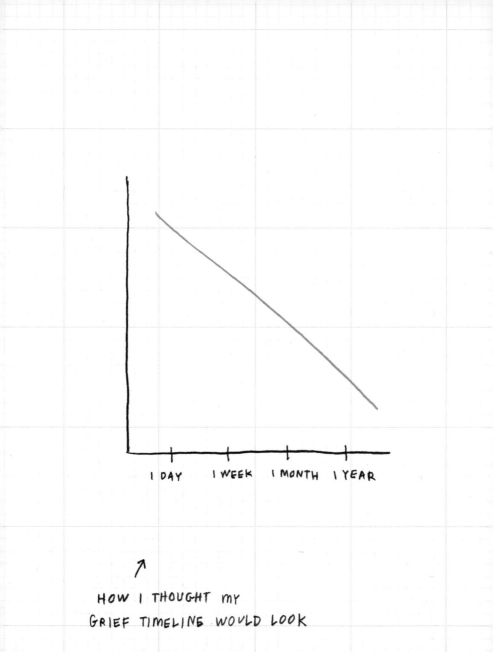

1 DAY   1 WEEK   1 MONTH   1 YEAR

HOW I THOUGHT MY
GRIEF TIMELINE WOULD LOOK

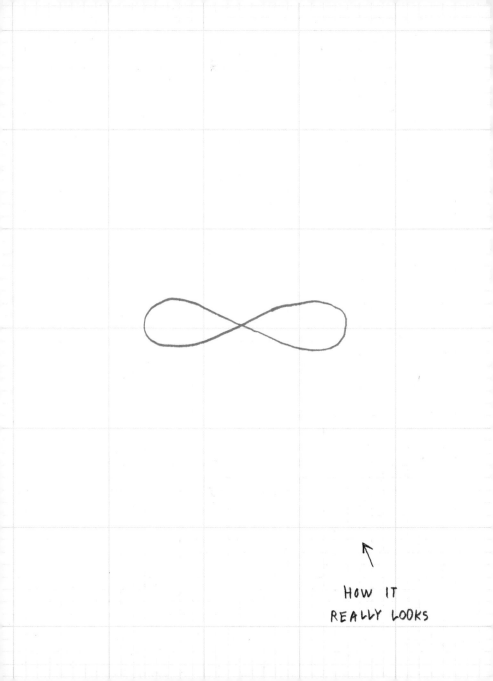

HOW IT
REALLY LOOKS

it's okay to take a break from
your grief.

there is a guilt that comes with loss,
a judgment that if you smile for a
second you don't care.

wanting to share
something with someone
who is no longer
in your life is
totally normal.

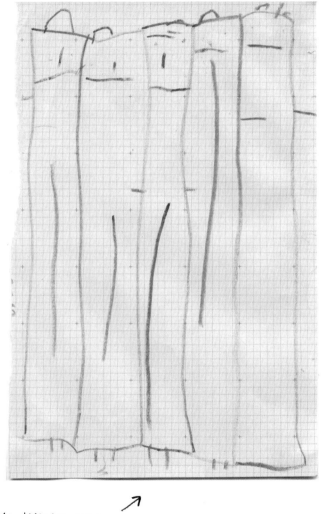

LOOK WHAT COCO
DREW, mom

SOMETIMES SHARING IS
JUST SHARING SPACE.

SOFTEN THROUGH THE EDGES.

the grief has not
gotten lighter, i'm
just learning how
to hold it a
little better.

EVEN THROUGH CLOUDY DAYS
FLOWERS STILL FOLLOW THE SUN.

HAPPINESS DOES NOT EQVAL
THE ABSENCE OF SADNESS.

i hurt,
but then i heal.
i cry,
but then i smile again.

this is the beauty
of being human.

part five:
continuing

THE SUN COMES UP
AND WE START AGAIN.

STEP BY

STEP BY

STEP BY

STEP BY

STEP BY

STEP

STEP BY

STEP BY

STEP BY

STEP BY

grief unfolds.

every turned page
reveals something new.

remember, we evolve.
explore your infinite possibility.

TODAY I SLOW DOWN AND
NOTICE THE SMALL THINGS.

IT'S COURAGE AND FEAR
NOT COURAGE OR FEAR

I WON'T GET OVER
THE LOSING
BUT I'VE LEARNED
MORE ABOUT LIVING
BECAUSE OF IT.

may you love and be loved.

may you love and be loved.

may you love and be loved

may you love and be loved.

may you love and be loved.

may you love and be loved

may you love and be love

with time, i'm learning that grief evolves,
you grow, and your relationship with it changes.
sometimes it's overwhelming,
sometimes it's a familiar old friend,

and sometimes all of that grief reminds you
how much you loved, or were loved.

DEAR MOM,

I SEE YOU
EVERYWHERE.

I MISS YOUR HANDS.

two years since i held your hand
and i feel myself soften into a pain
i know will never leave.

i'm learning to be gentle with my grief
in whatever form it shows up:
longing, guilt, regret, heartache,
it's all allowed to come and be cradled,
leave when it's ready.

some days are going to be ok,
and some days are not,
and that's ok too.

with time i realize that grief is not
something to overcome or complete,
rather a part of life and
a connection to my memories.

the continuing process has
given me perspective and wisdom,
and so much appreciation.

grief is love, adjusting.

thank you

margaret brown
heather corbett
soyolmaa lkhagvadorj
christina karem
tim matusch
andrew olanow
warren olanow
sasha stern
elizabeth sullivan
kate woodrow

and a special thank you
to roy chan
        +
my daughter, coco matusch
(your nana loved you so much)